Raising Student Aspirations

Classroom Activities
for Grades 9-12

Russell J. Quaglia and Kristine M. Fox

CONFIDENCE to TAKE ACTION

LEADERSHIP and RESPONSIBILITY

SPIRIT of ADVENTURE

CURIOSITY and CREATIVITY

FUN and EXCITEMENT

SENSE of ACCOMPLISHMENT

HEROES

BELONGING

Research Press 2612 North Mattis Avenue • Champaign, Illinois 61822 • [800] 519-2707 • www.researchpress.com

Composition by Jeff Helgesen
Cover design by Linda Brown, Positive I.D. Graphic Design, Inc.
Printed by McNaughton & Gunn, Inc.

ISBN 0-87822-482-3
Library of Congress Catalog Number 2002095760

Contents

Chapter 4: Fun and Excitement

Chapter 5: Curiosity and Creativity

Chapter 6: Spirit of Adventure

Chapter 7: Leadership and Responsibility

Chapter 8: Confidence to Take Action

Foreword

Creating supportive and personalized learning environments in which adolescents will feel connected to the school community is one of the demanding challenges facing secondary school administrators today. Such settings, many reports and studies have concluded, would improve student performance, significantly closing the "achievement gap"—a policy concern to educators that has become even more critical because of the "No Child Left Behind" legislation.

For these reasons, educators in search of meaningful, cogent guidance in addressing student motivation to achieve will find *Raising Student Aspirations* a valuable resource. Building rigorous, supportive, and personalized school environments is the substance of *Raising Student Aspirations*. By proposing meaningful activities that can be integrated into many areas of high school life, Russell Quaglia and Kristine Fox have created a powerful set of tools that will help foster a culture of respect, support, and care in which students will feel connected to their teachers and one another. This type of school culture is conducive to high performance because it provides a safe environment where change and improvement can take place.

Why is it so important to continue to try to change the culture of our schools? Certainly, in the past two decades, many educators have attempted to improve student achievement. Yet these efforts have produced uneven results, especially in high schools, where change has been more difficult to negotiate. One of the most persistent problems is the gap in student achievement, which exists across cultures, ethnicities, and economic classes. Another disappointing piece of data is the overall low achievement results of high school students on national tests. The National Assessment of Educational Progress (NAEP) test scores today show little or no progress in reading and science at the high school level. These various findings should bring into clear focus the need to energize the discourse on improving America's high schools.

By seeking to engage students in the learning process, the authors of *Raising Student Aspirations* tackle, in my view, the heart of high school improvement. The authors identify eight conditions essential to a school culture that foster success for all: Belonging, Heroes, and a Sense of Accomplishment will help raise student aspirations; Fun and Excitement, Curiosity and Creativity, and a Spirit of Adventure will cultivate enthusiasm; and Leadership and Responsibility and Confidence to Take Action will instill the courage to have higher aspirations. These conditions have the potential to erase inequities based on social status and cultural background. But how can teachers create these conditions for their students? *Raising Student Aspirations* provides them with the means to answer this question. I urge all secondary school principals to read *Raising Student Aspirations* and use it as a tool to energize their teachers in promoting equity and excellence for all secondary school students.

Gerald N. Tirozzi
Executive Director
National Association
   of Secondary School Principals

Introduction

As a teacher, you have the opportunity to create wonderful learning environments for your students every day. You have the power to make school an exciting, creative, and engaging place where students want to learn. Schools that support, understand, and truly believe in the potential of all students are on their way to developing a culture that supports student aspirations. Promoting student aspirations means that, as a teacher, you are inspiring your students to reach their full potential.

We have identified eight conditions that need to be in place in order for aspirations to flourish. These conditions are fostered through classroom activities, interactions, discussions, and school-wide initiatives. The eight conditions are as follows:

1. Belonging
2. Heroes
3. Sense of Accomplishment
4. Fun and Excitement
5. Curiosity and Creativity
6. Spirit of Adventure
7. Leadership and Responsibility
8. Confidence to Take Action

The activities in this book are designed to help you understand and promote these eight conditions. Although the conditions are described and meant to be introduced in your classroom in a set order, they also fit into three distinct categories.

Three Conditions That Serve as the Foundation for Raising Student Aspirations

The first condition is *belonging.* Belonging activities focus on helping students feel valued for their unique talents and interests. At the same time, these activities help to establish a community in your classroom. You should focus on establishing the condition of belonging the minute students enter the building on the first day of school. You should then continually support and reinforce this condition throughout the school year.

The second condition, *heroes,* focuses on helping students find at least one adult they can trust and turn to for advice. This adult serves as a hero by connecting with the student and promoting the student's desire to connect with others as well. Hero activities help students discover who the real heroes are in their lives, as well as understand that they, too, are heroes. Students who have high aspirations also have real heroes in their lives—people they can turn to for advice, support, and guidance.

The third condition, *sense of accomplishment,* promotes effort, perseverance, and good citizenship. Although academic achievement is critically important to students, there is more to learning than making the grade. Sense of accomplishment activities encourage students to put forth effort and persevere so that they will be successful in life as they mature into responsible citizens.

Three Conditions That Motivate Students and Instill Enthusiasm in the Classroom

The fourth condition is *fun and excitement*. Like the next two conditions, it focuses on the importance of making learning engaging for all students. Fun and excitement activities concentrate on helping students to enjoy school by teaching them to laugh while they learn. You will notice that students who find school exciting will also be engaged and interested in the learning process. They will feel motivated and enthusiastic about what you are teaching them.

The fifth condition, *curiosity and creativity,* is notable not only because it allows students to question and explore what they are learning, but also because it encourages them to remain inquisitive both inside and outside the classroom.

The sixth condition, *spirit of adventure,* has to do with your supporting students to take healthy risks, set goals for themselves, and not worry about failing. Activities that promote spirit of adventure encourage students to set high, achievable goals. Although students may fail in their first few attempts to take healthy risks and set meaningful goals, they can—with your help—learn to keep trying. By persevering, they will have captured the essence of the condition of spirit of adventure.

Two Conditions That Establish the Mind-Set Students Need in Order to Aspire

The seventh condition, *leadership and responsibility,* involves giving every student a voice in the learning environment. Leadership and responsibility activities teach students to be leaders and to work with others. All students have the potential to be leaders and to cooperate with those around them. What they need from you is your desire to teach them the necessary skills and to support them as they develop their unique leadership styles. With your help, they will acquire the mind-set they need in order to aspire.

The eighth condition, *confidence to take action,* relies on your encouraging students to believe in themselves and their abilities. Activities that promote confidence to take action support the development of your students' self-image and also acknowledge their special talents and wonderful contributions to your class, your school, and the world at large.

How the Eight Conditions Benefit Everyone

Supporting student aspirations in the classroom is both exciting and rewarding. As a teacher, you need to understand that promoting aspirations is not the same as implementing an add-on unit or a special program; rather, it is a way of thinking. Fostering aspirations in the classroom is about believing that all students deserve to be acknowledged, understood, cared about, and supported in all their wonderful endeavors.

The activities presented in this book are meant to enhance what great teachers do every day. Great teachers engage their students, have a passion for teaching and learning, and truly love the teaching profession. Keep in mind that these activities should be used to complement a school culture that already promotes and supports the development of student aspirations. It is hoped that these activities will help students and staff better understand the eight conditions that affect the development of their own aspirations.

The introduction of these activities in the classroom is a great way to begin raising student aspirations. Ideally, you, the teacher, should participate in these activities, too. Most of the activities can be done at any point in the school year, can be adapted for a variety of grade levels, and can be modified to suit the unique nature of your classroom.

We are well aware of the constant time pressures teachers face every day. We also know that investing time and energy in promoting student aspirations will have a positive effect on you, your students, and everyone in your school. These activities will breathe new life into your classroom and create an exciting learning environment. We hope you have fun with them as you help student aspirations flourish.

CHAPTER ONE

BELONGING

CONFIDENCE to TAKE ACTION

LEADERSHIP and RESPONSIBILITY

SPIRIT of ADVENTURE

CURIOSITY and CREATIVITY

FUN and EXCITEMENT

SENSE of ACCOMPLISHMENT

HEROES

BELONGING

ACTIVITY 1   On the Outside

To understand what it is like to be an outsider, it is important for students to comprehend the condition of belonging. A good way for them to gain an understanding of this condition is to put them in a situation in which they experience the feeling of being left out, of not being considered part of the crowd. This activity, which presupposes that your class consists of 25 students (one of whom will be estranged from the others), allows students to feel what it is like to be on the outside and to describe and discuss those feelings.

Materials ▶ Index cards and tape

Instructions 1. Before engaging students in this activity, think of five animals and write their names on index cards. If you have decided to use frogs, snakes, bears, cows, and rabbits, then you should divide students into groups of five and write each animal's name on the back of five index cards—except for one animal's name, which you should write on only four index cards. Then choose one lone animal and write its name on the back of the remaining card.

2. Tape an index card to each student's back. (Make sure that the student who winds up with the lone animal's name taped to his or her back is someone who has a strong sense of self.)

3. Tell the students that you need to divide them into groups in order for them to do a math activity. Have the students find their animal counterparts and assemble in their animal groups without speaking. Obviously, one student in the class will belong to none of the groups.

4. Once the students have formed their groups, ask them to come to you for their next set of directions. Give each group some instructions that are fairly easy to follow and perhaps funny. Assign the lone student a task more difficult than the others.

5. After a few minutes, call the entire class together and explain to them the purpose of the game. Encourage discussion by asking students the following questions:

      What was it like to find the others in your group?

      Did anyone notice that one student did not belong to any of the groups? How did you feel for that student?

      How did the student who had no group feel?

Discussion 1. How can we include students who are left out?

2. What would it feel like to always be on the outside?

3. What was it like to be part of a group?

Enrichment Challenge students not to leave anyone on the outside. At the end of each week, ask students to share how they helped one person be part of a group or a conversation.

ACTIVITY 2   Say It through a Song

Students of all ages love to listen to and learn through music. There have been many songs throughout history that have been used to unite a group or country. These songs have much power and meaning.

Materials
- A CD player
- CDs of songs—patriotic, antislavery, ethnic, and so forth—that have helped to unite groups of people through the ages
- News articles and books relating to the music

Instructions

1. Inform students that the class is going to spend some time throughout the week listening to music.
2. Each day, play a song or two that, throughout history, have been used to unite various groups of people.
3. Ask students to write down their thoughts and ideas about the songs. Encourage them to ponder why these songs helped to unite people and why people often use songs to unite a group.
4. Supplement the songs with news articles or books about the time periods in which the songs were written.

Discussion

1. Why do you enjoy listening to music?
2. What songs have influenced you to unite with a group or organization?
3. Why do you think music is often important for groups?

Enrichment

Ask your students to write a new class or school song. Be sure the song reflects the identity of the student body and the history of the school.

ACTIVITY 3   Stereotypes

Understanding and celebrating diversity are important if students are to embrace the condition of belonging. Diversity comes in many forms, and the more students experience diversity, the better they can understand the concept. This activity allows students to feel what it is like to wear different labels and understand the stereotypes that accompany those labels.

Materials

▶ Stereotype Cards

▶ Tape

Instructions

1. Select six students, have them tape one of the Stereotype Cards to the front of their shirt or dress, and then have them sit in front of the class.

2. Ask the rest of the students to discuss the traits they believe these students possess.

3. List these traits on the chalkboard next to the names of the students wearing the Stereotype Cards.

4. Depending on the makeup of your class, you may want to continue this activity throughout the morning, instructing the rest of the class to treat these students the way they would normally treat people who are similarly stereotyped.

5. Follow up with discussion and conversation; they are essential to the success of this activity.

Discussion

1. How does it feel to be stereotyped?

2. Why do we assign labels to people who are different from us?

3. How can we as a class do away with labels and stereotypes?

Enrichment

Ask students to talk with their parents about the stereotypes prevalent in their generation: What have they learned about the people they once stereotyped?

How has this country stereotyped people, and what has been the effect of these stereotypes?

Stereotype Cards

Jock

Dummy

Nerd

Egghead

Computer geek

Idiot

Raising Student Aspirations: Classroom Activities for Grades 9–12
© 2003 by Russell J. Quaglia and Kristine M. Fox. Champaign, IL: Research Press (800) 519-2707

One way to imbue students with a sense of belonging is to allow them to have more of a say in the development of their courses and curriculum. Students who feel ownership and responsibility for their learning are more likely to participate and attend classes. This activity helps students feel more involved in the learning process.

Materials   ▶ Writing paper and pencils or pens

Instructions   1. Choose either a new unit or a unit that you would like to teach differently.

2. Let students know the unit objectives or desired outcomes.

3. Allow students the opportunity to develop various methods of reaching the learning outcomes.

4. You may initially have to prompt the students with several choices. After you do this with one unit, the students will quickly rise to the challenge and look forward to having their opinions heard when you come to another unit.

Discussion   1. What did you learn about lesson development?

2. How difficult was it to create a lesson that interested all students?

3. If you were given the choice to learn about anything, what would it be and why?

Enrichment   Give your students the opportunity to develop various assessment tools for a lesson they created. Ask students to help with the grading.

Give your students the opportunity to teach a lesson. Make sure to help prepare them by letting them do a trial run. The goal of this enrichment activity is to have students experience a positive teaching experience.

ACTIVITY 5   Student-Parent Conferences

Once their children enter high school, parents typically spend less time discussing their children's progress and getting to know what they are learning on a daily basis. This activity helps parents become more involved in their children's education.

Materials ► Report cards

Instructions

1. Rather than just sending parents their children's report cards, ask parents and students to come to the school twice a year to meet and discuss the report cards.

2. Be sure to have students discuss their work and their grades so that you are not doing all the explaining yourself.

3. Help the students set goals for the next grading period.

4. If some parents are unable to attend a meeting, arrange for a conference call so you can still engage parent and student in the same conversation at the same time.

Discussion

1. What improvements do you need to make before the next grading period?

2. What can the school do to help provide you with better support?

3. How can teachers and the school as a whole better communicate with your parents?

Enrichment

At the end of each grading period, ask your students to grade you as a teacher: What units did they like or dislike? How could the class be improved in the future? Did the students think the tests and homework were fair? Why or why not?

ACTIVITY 6   Mood Cards

Anyone who has taught high school is familiar with the wide range of moods that students bring to the classroom every day. Their lives are filled with ups and downs, and the classroom is often the last place they want to be, as their minds often wander. Regardless of what occurs outside the building, students need to know that they are accepted and welcomed at school. They need to view school as a safe place both physically and emotionally. This activity should help reinforce that view. It is an activity you may decide to do randomly throughout the month, especially when you know that the students are feeling stressed, tired, or anxious.

Materials
- ▶ Mood Cards
- ▶ Index cards (for making additional Mood Cards for the entire class)

Instructions
1. Before the start of class, spread out the Mood Cards on a desk or table near the door of the classroom.
2. As they enter the room, ask the students to choose one of the Mood Cards.
3. Let your students know that you are well aware that they come to class in different moods and that, regardless, you respect their feelings.
4. Have students place their Mood Card on their desk.
5. Comment on some of the moods represented on the cards and explore why students chose a specific Mood Card.
6. Explain to students that, by understanding each other's moods, they can better support each other and also work together more effectively.
7. You, too, should select a Mood Card and then explain to the class why you are in that particular mood.

Discussion
1. Why do some people always seem to be in a bad mood?
2. Are moods innate or learned?
3. How can we help others who are in a bad mood?

Enrichment
Encourage students to keep a journal of their moods. They may find that on certain mornings they are in a bad mood on the way to school, but on other mornings they are in a good mood, especially when they pass their friends in the hallway.

Mood Cards

Depressed	Happy
Sad	Angry
Mad	Excited
Optimistic	Pessimistic
Eager	Anxious
Hopeful	Alert
Lazy	Energetic

Raising Student Aspirations: Classroom Activities for Grades 9–12
© 2003 by Russell J. Quaglia and Kristine M. Fox. Champaign, IL: Research Press (800) 519-2707

ACTIVITY 7   Physical and Mental Stretches

In the wacky world of high school, students often are unable to take the time to regain their composure as they rush from class to class. Students are expected to rush to their lockers, rush down the hall, and then rush to class. This activity helps students refocus their energy.

Materials ► None

Instructions

1. Develop a variety of quick stretches, both physical and mental.

2. As your students enter the room and take their seats, ask them to engage in either a physical stretch or a mental stretch. (A mental stretch would be an exercise that helps students clear their minds of the previous class's activities or of the hustle and bustle in the hallways between classes.)

3. The stretching exercise should take only a few minutes, but it will help get everyone on the same page. It is important that you participate in the stretching exercise as well.

4. As the year progresses, give students the responsibility of leading the class in stretching before engaging in classroom work.

Discussion

1. What methods do you use to help you focus and concentrate?

2. How do physical activities help us mentally?

3. Are there other quick, creative ways we could start our class?

Enrichment Together with your students, develop a "mind" guide for other classes to use. The guide should highlight various stretches and explain the purpose of beginning class this way. Incorporate student input and stories.

Scenarios for Belonging

Read the following scenarios to your students one at a time. After you have read each scenario, give students ample time to think about their responses to it and then engage them in a lively class discussion.

1. It is the third month of school. A new student enters your school. She has a heavy accent and dresses differently from the other students. You and your friends are asked to help welcome this student to your school and town. What do you do to make her feel that she belongs?

2. You are a freshman and are trying out for the soccer team. You make the team, but two of your friends do not. They are upset and no longer want to hang with you. What do you do?

3. The new principal just instituted a policy that students are no longer allowed to hang around school before the start of the school day or after the end of the school day. You may enter the building when the bell rings and must leave right after school. How do you approach this issue?

4. You have been the victim of a nasty false rumor. Throughout the school day, other students are snickering and laughing at you. You think people are starting to believe the rumor. What do you do?

Challenge Activities for Belonging

For Students
- ► Challenge students to stop spreading rumors and negative talk about their classmates. Have them try to diffuse rumors and even say positive things about other students they may not like.
- ► Challenge students to say hello to a student they usually do not even notice.
- ► Challenge students to introduce themselves to adults in the building they do not know, such as custodial staff, cafeteria workers, and teachers from different classrooms.

For Teachers
- ► Take the time to talk to your students in the hallway, in the cafeteria, or at after-school events.
- ► Stop in and visit another teacher's classroom. Arrange to have a substitute take over your class so you can learn what other classes do on a daily basis.
- ► Hang around the entranceway when the school day begins and ends. Take the time to say hello to students as the school day begins and welcome them to school.

CHAPTER TWO

HEROES

CONFIDENCE to TAKE ACTION

LEADERSHIP and RESPONSIBILITY

SPIRIT of ADVENTURE

CURIOSITY and CREATIVITY

FUN and EXCITEMENT

SENSE of ACCOMPLISHMENT

HEROES

BELONGING

ACTIVITY 1　　　Our Graduates

Students are often surprised when they hear about the wonderful achievements of graduates from their own school. Usually, once students graduate from high school, they are forgotten unless they do indeed achieve something newsworthy. This activity gives students an opportunity to dig deep into their school's history, discover its heroes, and honor them and their accomplishments by creating an alumni wall.

Materials
- Stationery, writing paper, and pencils or pens
- Tape or thumbtacks

Instructions
1. Inform your students that they are going to create an alumni wall.
2. Have students gather information about several high-achieving graduates from their school who are not friends or relatives. Tell students they may have to do a bit of work in order to track these people down.
3. Make sure you encourage the students to research alumni from all different generations.
4. Once they have located their alumni, have the students write letters to them, explaining the project and asking them for interviews.
5. Tell students that, during their interviews, they should ask the alumni what they have been doing since high school.
6. Have students write their subjects' biographies and post them on the alumni wall with tape or thumbtacks. Encourage students to think of a creative title for the display.

Discussion
1. What is the most interesting thing you learned about the alumni you chose?
2. What would you like your alumni biography to say?
3. What surprised you about your alumni?

Enrichment
Create an alumni Web site, where alumni can register and find each other. Notify the alumni of the Web site once it has been created.

ACTIVITY 2   Historical Heroes

As soon as they enter kindergarten, students are introduced to heroes. Heroes represent our culture, our values, and our history. Although there are many kinds of heroes, most students are familiar only with famous heroes. This activity provides students with a better understanding of what constitutes a hero.

Materials
- History and social studies textbooks
- Writing paper and pencils or pens

Instructions

1. Begin by discussing the topic of heroes with your students and ask them to think about all the historical heroes they have learned about in school. List these heroes on the chalkboard.
2. Discuss with your students the reasons these people are heroes.
3. Inform your class that their next writing assignment will involve researching and learning about a historical hero whom most people have never heard of.
4. Once they have completed their assignment, have students share their research with the class. You, too, should participate in this project.

Discussion

1. What makes someone a hero?
2. What are some common characteristics of heroes?
3. Do you know anyone who will be a hero sometime in the future?

Enrichment

Ask students to explore historical heroes from their town or community. They may have to conduct interviews or explore the archives of the town hall or library.

Encourage your students to research a hero from a different country or ethnic background.

ACTIVITY 3   Family Heroes

All families have heroes. A family hero may be a parent, a sibling, or a great-grandparent. Students often express amazement when they discover that their family tree includes heroes. This activity gives students pause to consider how they themselves can be heroes to their family every day.

Materials

► Writing paper and pencils or pens

Instructions

1. Ask students to think about as many relatives as they can. For some students this will be easier than it is for others.

2. Tell students their task is to learn about a hero from their family. The hero may be someone from the distant past or someone who is still alive.

3. Encourage students to share their family hero with the class however they choose, including through videos, newspaper clippings, songs, poems, and so forth.

4. Encourage students to share their hero projects with their family.

Discussion

1. Fifty years from now, if your grandchildren are asked to write about their grandparent as a hero, what do you hope they say about you?

2. How can you be a hero to your family every day?

3. What surprised you the most about the hero in your family?

Enrichment

Have students create a family tree and list why each member of their family is a hero in one way or another. (Prior to doing this activity, make sure you know your class well; this activity would be inappropriate for students who are unsure of or embarrassed about their backgrounds.) Another option is to have students brainstorm how they are heroes every day.

ACTIVITY 4   Person of the Year

It is important for people of all ages to recognize important figures who have made a difference locally, nationally, or globally. There are many unsung heroes whose lives and generosity are worth learning about. This activity helps students do just that.

Materials
▶ Current newspapers and magazines
▶ Drawing paper and markers

Instructions
1. Discuss with your students the annual issue of *Time* magazine in which the publication's person of the year is featured on the cover and in the text: Mention the names of some of *Time*'s past choices and be aware that some of these people may not be familiar to your students. Take some time to discuss these famous people's accomplishments and the reasons they were chosen for the cover of the magazine.

2. Ask students to think about whom they would select as the next person of the year. Be sure to give students enough time to research those candidates they deem qualified to receive the honor.

3. Have students create a front cover for the magazine and give their reasons for choosing this person. Depending on the makeup of your class, you may also want to participate in this project.

Discussion
1. What makes a person's life important?
2. What was the most interesting thing you learned while doing this project?
3. What accomplishment would you like to be recognized for someday?

Enrichment
Assign students the task of learning about past people of the year chosen by *Time:* Do you agree with the selections? What type of long-term impact did that person have on society? Has this honor been bestowed equitably on different people from different countries? If not, who has not been fairly represented?

ACTIVITY 5	My Hero

Without their realizing it, adults and high school students often are heroes to people. For example, the student you say hello to or the neighbor you occasionally help may see you as a hero. Heroes love to know that they are making a difference and that you appreciate their efforts. This activity encourages students to take the time to recognize someone who has made a difference in their lives.

Materials
- ▶ Drawing paper, markers, and pencils or pens
- ▶ Envelopes and postage

Instructions
1. Begin by discussing the topic of heroes with your students. Ask students to think of heroes who are neither famous nor rich.
2. As a class, create hero stationery. You may want to hold a contest and then choose the best stationery, or you may want each student to create his or her own stationery.
3. Have students send a letter of thanks to someone they consider a hero. Encourage students to think of heroes other than friends or relatives—people who have no idea of the positive effect they are having on students.
4. Once they have finished their thank-you letters, have the students mail them.

Discussion
1. Why is it powerful to receive a note of appreciation?
2. How have you been recognized for your heroic acts?
3. What else can we do to recognize the heroes in our lives?

Enrichment
Each month, give students the opportunity to recognize someone important to them. The recognition may take the form of a card, a letter, a phone call, or even an invitation to lunch in the cafeteria.

At the end of the school year, invite the heroes in for a celebration and group recognition.

ACTIVITY 6   Stand and Deliver

Heroes believe in the potential of their protégés. Teachers who are heroes, for example, have high expectations for the students they work with, and they dream about the wonderful future that lies ahead for those students. A true hero never gives up, even in the face of major obstacles and seemingly overwhelming odds.

Materials
- ► A video about a hero, such as *Stand and Deliver,* and a VCR
- ► A nonfiction story about a hero

Instructions
1. Discuss with students a number of movies, books, and poems that have been created about everyday heroes.
2. During the course of one month, use a variety of sources to introduce and discuss the topic of heroes with your students. *Stand and Deliver,* for example, is a movie that most students can relate to in one way or another.
3. After discussing the topic of heroes and showing the video to the class, have the students read a nonfiction story about a hero.

Discussion
1. Why was the main character in the movie or the book a hero?
2. What was the hero's best quality and why?
3. Would this person be a hero today? Why or why not?

Enrichment   Ask students to create their own heroic stories based on the life of someone they know. Have students interview and videotape people whenever possible.

ACTIVITY 7   I Am a Hero

It is important for students to understand that we all need heroes and that they themselves are or have been heroes to others. Students often do not realize the effect they have on people's lives because they find it difficult to make an honest assessment of their assets and their strengths. This activity helps students learn to appreciate themselves as heroes.

Materials
- ▶ Writing paper and pencils or pens

Instructions

1. Ask students to take a few moments to think about someone who views them as a hero. Some students may say that no one looks up to or admires them. Encourage these students to think about what they have done for their siblings or even their parents and grandparents.

2. Have students write a letter of thanks to themselves. The letter should explain how they have been a hero and why they have made a difference in others' lives.

Discussion

1. What makes someone a positive hero?
2. How can heroes have a negative influence? Explain.
3. Can you recall a time when you admired a negative hero?

Enrichment

Have students create a collage of photos, drawings, or words representing how they have been a hero to someone.

Scenarios for Heroes

Read the following scenarios to your students one at a time. After you have read each scenario, give students ample time to think about their responses to it and then engage them in a lively class discussion.

1. Students in the elementary school admire a particular high school student. The high school student is a great athlete and well known throughout the town. This student also has been known to cheat and shoplift whenever possible. What can you do about this situation?

2. Your best friend has just been cut from the soccer team. She worked harder than you all summer. She won't speak to you and is upset that you made the team. How can you be a hero to your friend?

3. Throughout history negative leaders have been heroes to people. People have followed cult leaders, murderers, thieves. Why are these people seen as heroes? How do you deal with the negative heroes at your school and in your life?

4. A teacher you really admire has been unfair to one of your classmates. The student was suspended for cheating, and you know he did not cheat. The teacher says she is not going to listen to any more arguments and that the decision has been made. What do you do?

Challenge Activities for Heroes

For Students   ▶ Encourage students to take the time to thank teachers or coaches who have been heroes to them. Have them let these people know they have made a difference in their lives.

▶ Challenge students to be heroes to younger students. Suggest that they play games with these younger students at recess or just hang out with them.

▶ Have students get to know some veterans of war who live in their community. Encourage students to thank these veterans for their service to their country.

For Teachers   ▶ Attend some of your students' after-school events, such as basketball games, school plays, or choir performances.

▶ Be a hero to your colleagues. Take the time to recognize the hard work they do. Visit their classrooms, look at their displays, and ask about their projects.

▶ Mentor a new teacher. Help the teacher learn more about the school and the profession.

CHAPTER THREE

SENSE of ACCOMPLISHMENT

CONFIDENCE to TAKE ACTION

LEADERSHIP and RESPONSIBILITY

SPIRIT of ADVENTURE

CURIOSITY and CREATIVITY

FUN and EXCITEMENT

SENSE of ACCOMPLISHMENT

HEROES

BELONGING

ACTIVITY 1   Our Community

It is hoped that, by the time students reach high school, they will have been introduced to the idea of community service. Unfortunately, most students partake in community service projects only randomly throughout the school year. This activity encourages students to get involved and stay involved for an entire year.

Materials   ▶ None

Instructions   1. Together with your students, spend some time learning about the community you live in: What are the community's greatest assets? What would help make it a better place to live?

2. After gathering the necessary information, decide on a class project. The project will take much planning and effort, but the rewards should be great.

3. Make sure all students have a role in the planning and implementation of the community service project.

Discussion   1. Why is it important to give something back to your community?

2. What has volunteering meant to you personally?

3. How else can we get involved in our community?

Enrichment   Encourage students to get involved with local politics. Perhaps they could attend a school board meeting or a town council meeting. Make sure to help students who are of voting age to get out and vote.

ACTIVITY 2   Perseverance

We all want our students to try harder and persevere when they confront a challenge they perceive as overwhelming. As difficult as it is to teach, however, the concept of perseverance is one that students must grasp. This activity gives students pause to consider the importance of perseverance in their lives.

Materials   ► Some famous quotes and a few interesting, sometimes forgotten historical facts

Instructions   1. Inform students that you are going to read a few famous quotes and that you would like to hear what they have to say about them.

2. Read the following to your students:

   "History has demonstrated that the most notable winners usually encountered heartbreaking obstacles before they triumphed. They won because they refused to become discouraged by their defeats." (B. C. Forbes)

   John Milton became blind at the age of 44. Sixteen years later he wrote the classic *Paradise Lost.*

   Abraham Lincoln entered the Blackhawk War as a captain. By the end of the war, he had been demoted to the rank of private.

   Leon Uris, author of the best-seller *Exodus,* failed high school English three times.

3. Have students think back to a time in their life when they had to persevere to be successful. Give students enough time to share their stories with the class.

Discussion   1. How does one learn to persevere?

2. What other stories of perseverance are you familiar with?

3. In what academic areas would the ability to persevere help you?

Enrichment   Encourage students to search for other stories about perseverance. These stories are readily available in weekly magazines and papers. What common traits do they find among people who persevere against all odds?

ACTIVITY 3   My Country

Good citizenship is an important component of the condition of sense of accomplishment, and it can take many forms. It may mean taking part in community service, going to the polls to vote on election day, or being a good neighbor. It is hoped that all students who graduate from high school have had the opportunity to display good citizenship skills.

Materials   ▶ Writing paper and pencils or pens

Instructions   1. Hold a short discussion about citizenship with your students: What does a good citizen do on a daily basis? What are our responsibilities as good citizens?

2. Ask students to think about their favorite aspects of their country of origin.

3. Ask students to think about one aspect of their country that they would like to change.

4. Help students draft a letter to their congressperson or other elected representative. The letter should address their concern and ask for a response.

5. Make sure students understand how important their voice is in the political process.

Discussion   1. In what ways can we have our voices heard as citizens?

2. How have you seen a small group of people make a big difference?

3. How can teenagers get more involved in issues that concern them?

Enrichment   Help your students write letters to the editor of the local newspaper when an issue concerns or affects them.

Try to have every student write at least one editorial during the school year that he or she would like to see published in the newspaper.

ACTIVITY 4   My Achievements

Students often fail to realize that they achieve wonderful things every day. Perhaps they were sick during the weekend but still managed to finish their homework. Maybe they worked one or two after-school jobs during the week and still kept up with their studies. Achievements cannot and should not be measured merely by test grades. Achievements include myriad student accomplishments and efforts. Most high schools do a good job of recognizing academic achievements. This activity helps teachers and students recognize other forms of achievement.

Materials
► My Accomplishments Worksheet
► Pencils or pens

Instructions
1. Hold a short discussion about all the things we do that are not related to academics. For example, students may work after school, participate in sports, build or create something as part of a hobby, or receive an award from an organization that is not tied to the school.
2. Give students the My Accomplishments Worksheet and have them list three accomplishments in each column. Remind them that accomplishments do not relate only to academics.
3. After students have completed the worksheet, ask them to turn it over and write three things they have accomplished so far today.
4. Ask students to give themselves a round of applause for all their accomplishments. Have students pair up and share a few of their accomplishments with their partners.
5. Have students then share a few of their partners' accomplishments with the rest of the class.

Discussion
1. Why is it important to celebrate all types of accomplishments?
2. What surprised you about your accomplishments during the past year?
3. Aside from handing out grades, how else should the school recognize student accomplishments?

Enrichment
Ask students to think about all they have accomplished since they entered school. These accomplishments may include learning to read or write, solving math problems, or even making friends.

Ask students to think about the two most important accomplishments of their lives thus far.

My Accomplishments Worksheet

My Accomplishments This Week

1. _____
   _____
   _____

2. _____
   _____
   _____

3. _____
   _____
   _____

My Accomplishments This Month

1. _____
   _____
   _____

2. _____
   _____
   _____

3. _____
   _____
   _____

My Accomplishments This Year

1. _____
   _____
   _____

2. _____
   _____
   _____

3. _____
   _____
   _____

Raising Student Aspirations: Classroom Activities for Grades 9–12 © 2003 by Russell J. Quaglia and Kristine M. Fox. Champaign, IL: Research Press (800) 519-2707

ACTIVITY 5　　Try This!

Sometimes students need to experience the rewards of perseverance before they can fully appreciate what it feels like to be successful. Any activity that challenges students to think and make several attempts before being successful will enhance student understanding of perseverance. This activity is both challenging and fun.

Materials
- ► 1 hula hoop, several basketballs, and 1 jump rope
- ► Several questions that are neither too easy nor too difficult to answer correctly
- ► 25 sheets of construction paper
- ► Tape

Instructions
1. Inform students that they are going to participate in fun activities in the gym that may require several attempts before they can be completed successfully.
2. Divide the class into five groups.
3. Set up five stations in the gym so that each station is geared toward one of the five activities described below.
4. Let the class know that each group is going to visit five stations, and that each student in the group is going to have to complete the required tasks. Remind students not to get frustrated if it takes longer than expected for each group member to finish an activity.
5. Randomly select the order in which each group will begin visiting the five stations. Tell students that, once the first group has completed the required task at the first station, the next group can begin, and so on.
6. Have students complete the following tasks:

   At the first station, give the group a hula hoop. Have the students form a human chain and pass the hula hoop from one end to the other without dropping it and without breaking the chain. This activity must be completed in 1 minute (or in whatever amount of time that seems reasonable for your students).

   At the second station, give each student a basketball to throw backwards (over the head) until it goes through the hoop. Everyone must make a basket before the group can advance to the next station.

   At the third station, ask each student to answer one of the questions you have prepared in advance. The group cannot move to the next station until everyone has correctly answered the question posed to him or her.

   At the fourth station, have two members of the group swing the jump rope in circles as the other students try to jump over it one at a time. At some point, the two students who are swinging the rope will have to turn that chore over to two other students and then jump the rope themselves. Once everyone has succeeded at this task, the group can move to the last station.

At the fifth—and final—station, give the group 25 sheets of paper and an adequate supply of tape. Have the students build the highest freestanding building possible. This task will require teamwork and good communication.

7. Congratulate the students when they make it through all five stations and then spend some time discussing perseverance.

Discussion

1. What did your group do when you had a disagreement?
2. Which activity required the most perseverance?
3. What school subject requires the most perseverance for you to be successful at?

Enrichment

Once a month, lead your students through an adventure activity. Each activity should require students to try doing it several times before they do it correctly and should also require them to work together. Whenever possible, take your students outside to do their activity.

Retirement Award

Thinking about the future can be overwhelming for anyone. It is precisely for that reason that high school students need to spend some time thinking about what they would like to accomplish by the time they reach certain milestones in their lives. This activity will help them plan for the future now rather than later.

Materials   ▶ Writing paper and pencils or pens

Instructions   1. Inform students that they are going to be attending their own retirement party, at which time they will be receiving a lifetime achievement award.

2. Tell the class that, in order for the presenter of the award to know about their accomplishments, they must help out by writing their autobiography. Even though they have yet to experience the future, they will have to write about themselves as though they already have. They do need a few reminders, though:

> They should focus on what they accomplished by the time they reached certain milestones, such as ages 21, 30, 40, 50, and 65 (the latter presumably being retirement age).

> They should do their writing alone and not share any of their accomplishments with their classmates.

> They should refrain from writing their names at the top of the page or providing any hints as to their identity anywhere in the autobiography.

3. After the students have written their stories (and possibly buttressed them with illustrations), collect them and then distribute them to the class, making sure that each student receives someone else's autobiography.

4. Have each student read to the class the story he or she has been given, and see if the class can guess whose autobiography is being read.

Discussion   1. Did you learn anything new about yourself when you thought about the future?

2. What are some possible ways for you to begin realizing your dreams?

3. What else would you like to add to your future?

Enrichment   Ask students to create a collage that they feel represents their future. This collage should consist of only a few material things they someday wish to own. More important, it should portray the kind of persons they want to be and also answer questions about themselves such as the following: What kind of life do I want to lead? Where do I want to live? What groups or organizations do I want to belong to or be associated with?

ACTIVITY 7   Good Citizenship through Writing

People feel wonderful when they do good deeds in the community and behave as good citizens. So, too, do students who help others in school. Many opportunities for exhibiting good citizenship exist in the schools, such as the one described in this activity: older students creating books for younger students.

Materials
► Loose-leaf writing paper and pencils or pens
► Loose-leaf notebooks
► Drawing paper and markers

Instructions
1. Acquire a list of first and second graders, along with as much information about them as possible, such as their favorite color or animal or food or activity.

2. Once you have collected as many names as there are students in your own high school class, let your students know that their next writing assignment is to create a personal book (in the form of a loose-leaf notebook) for a younger student.

3. Give each of your students the name and short bio of a first or second grader.

4. Encourage the class to write creative, exciting, and unique stories, using their "adopted" student's name as the central character and then incorporating as many facts about that student as possible.

5. Once the masterpieces are finished, invite the younger students to your class to receive their books.

Discussion
1. In one word, what was your adopted student's reaction to his or her book?

2. Why do you think the younger kids look up to you?

3. How can we continue to be good citizens to our younger students?

Enrichment
Develop a mentoring or reading program in which older students read to younger students on a monthly basis. Pair up the older students with the same younger students each month.

Read the following scenarios to your students one at a time. After you have read each scenario, give students ample time to think about their responses to it and then engage them in a lively class discussion.

1. You have been working on your English assignment for weeks. You thought it was very good and you put forth much effort. The grade you get is much worse than you anticipated. What do you do?

2. It is common knowledge that students cheat on math exams. Students plug information into their calculators and use it as an aid when they take their tests. You are finding this frustrating and cannot understand how the teacher does not know. What do you do?

3. You spent all summer working out and training in hopes of making the football team. After two weeks of tryouts, your name is on the list to be cut. You never even considered not making the team. Your effort and hard work seem not to have been worth it. What do you do?

4. One of your teachers uses only a single test score to evaluate your learning comprehension for the entire semester. You think this is unfair because you are a poor test taker. Your teacher is willing to listen to your suggestions and ideas. Make your case.

Challenge Activities for Sense of Accomplishment

For Students
- ► Challenge students to rewrite a paper or redo an exam, even though they don't feel like doing it. Have them take the opportunity to improve the quality of their work.

- ► Encourage students to get involved in a community service project. Have them gather a group of friends and find a project they can do together.

- ► Challenge students not to allow themselves to wait until the last minute to begin and complete projects. Challenge them to do this for an entire month. Suggest that they tell themselves the deadline is early and that, on the day before the assignment is due, they should take the time to revise, edit, and improve their project.

For Teachers
- ► Even if their grades do not improve, recognize your students' effort and perseverance. Let students know that you appreciate their hard work.

- ► Volunteer to help out at a school dance or function. Be a role model for community service by volunteering in your school community.

- ► Put forth a little extra effort and create new and exciting lesson plans each week. The lessons should be engaging and stimulating for students. Teach in a way that surprises your students.

CHAPTER FOUR

FUN and EXCITEMENT

CONFIDENCE to TAKE ACTION

LEADERSHIP and RESPONSIBILITY

SPIRIT of ADVENTURE

CURIOSITY and CREATIVITY

FUN and EXCITEMENT

SENSE of ACCOMPLISHMENT

HEROES

BELONGING

ACTIVITY 1   Political Cartoons

Bringing fun and excitement into the high school classroom is of the utmost importance because students who are bored are less likely to be engaged or even attend class. When students are excited about what is happening in the classroom, they feel free to laugh, and they also see that learning can be fun. This activity shows how the classroom can be transformed from a dull workplace into a lively learning environment.

Materials
► A variety of political cartoons
► Drawing paper and colored pencils or pens
► Tape or thumbtacks
► Optional: a folder or other casing that can be used for a portfolio

Instructions
1. Divide students into groups of three. Give each group of students three or four political cartoons to analyze.
2. Have students discuss the humor and irony they find in the cartoons and what messages the cartoonists are trying to convey.
3. Ask students to create their own cartoons and tell them that their cartoons should convey a message. To help them get started, you may suggest, for example, that they create cartoons that satirize state or local issues. Make sure you give the students time to draw and color their cartoons.
4. Display the cartoons by taping or tacking them to the walls of the classroom or placing them in a portfolio.

Discussion
1. What makes a cartoon funny?
2. How do cartoonists depict powerful people, wealthy people, actors, and others? What stereotypes do they depict?
3. What current topics would you like to see depicted in cartoons? Why?

Enrichment
Invite a cartoonist to speak with your class about his or her occupation: What training does it take to become a cartoonist? How do cartoonists get their ideas? What is the favorite political cartoon of the classroom visitor? Have any of his or her cartoons met with negative reactions?

ACTIVITY 2   A Hat Full of Fun

Spontaneity helps to promote the condition of fun and excitement in the classroom. Because routines eventually become boring for students, anything that adds a bit of excitement and interest to the routine of homework will help promote learning. This activity should help make homework assignments more palatable.

Materials
- Slips of paper with homework assignments listed on them
- A hat

Instructions

1. Once a month, create five or six unique homework assignments and list them on the slips of paper. Because you will be creating only a few assignments, you will need to list each one several times so that there are enough slips for each student. (Obviously, several students will wind up working on the same assignment. Make sure, however, that you know which assignment each student has selected.)

2. Put the slips of paper in the hat and have each student draw one slip. Depending on the class you teach, the assignments will vary, as the following examples show:

   In math class, you might ask that the student complete only problems 1–10 or 10–30 or maybe just one problem on a certain page in the textbook.

   In English class, you might create five assignments that relate to the same topic but that give different instructions on how to reach the same objective.

3. Another way to bring fun and excitement to homework is to allow students the opportunity to create their own homework assignments or think of different methods of reaching the objectives you have outlined.

Discussion

1. What homework assignments did you have fun completing? Why?
2. How can we make homework more interesting?
3. How should homework be graded?

Enrichment

Take the time to evaluate the homework you currently are assigning your students. Is it interesting to them? Is it serving as a valuable learning experience?

Seek student input in creating homework assignments. On a rotating basis, have several students a week help come up with homework assignments.

ACTIVITY 3   Rooting Out Boredom

One comment that teachers often hear from students is "I'm so bored." This activity helps students understand the roots of their boredom and the ways they can eliminate it during the school day. In the process, it also gives students some responsibility for overcoming their boredom.

Materials
- ▶ Rooting Out Boredom Worksheet
- ▶ Pencils or pens

Instructions

1. Give students the Rooting Out Boredom Worksheet and have them list their activities in the appropriate columns.

2. Tell students that, before they continue filling out the worksheet, they should think seriously about school—their experiences during an average school day, the classes they take, the homework assignments they complete, and so on. Only then should they complete the worksheet. Encourage students to really think about what makes activities boring or fun.

3. Have students share their ideas with the class.

4. Ask students how they can make boring activities more fun: How can they take responsibility for making the school day fun and exciting?

Discussion

1. What types of boring activities were most commonly mentioned by classmates?

2. What can we do as a class to reduce boredom?

3. How can learning be more exciting?

Enrichment

Solicit student input before designing some of your lessons. In other words, what do students want to learn from a specific unit?

Find ways to capitalize on student interests and strengths.

Rooting Out Boredom Worksheet

Boring Activities	Fun and Exciting Activities
1. _____	1. _____
_____	_____
2. _____	2. _____
_____	_____
3. _____	3. _____
_____	_____
4. _____	4. _____
_____	_____
5. _____	5. _____
_____	_____
6. _____	6. _____
_____	_____

What makes these activities boring?

_____

_____

_____

_____

_____

_____

_____

What makes these activities fun and exciting?

_____

_____

_____

_____

_____

_____

_____

| ACTIVITY 4 | **Sharing Assessment** |

Student assessment may not appear to be a fun and exciting topic, but it has the potential to be interesting—especially if you provide students with a variety of assessment opportunities. This activity shows how you can engage students in the assessment process.

Materials   ▶ Information about assessment

Instructions   1. Provide students with a variety of information about assessment. Tell them that, although it is traditional to assess students' knowledge by using fill-in-the-blank or multiple-choice tests, there are many other ways to test a student's mastery of a subject.

2. Together with your students, brainstorm nontraditional methods of assessment, such as skits, poems, essays, videos, 3-D art projects, students teaching students, and the like. You will find that many students are unaware of the many nontraditional ways that student work can be assessed.

3. At least once a month, allow students the opportunity to choose how their work will be assessed. Depending on the makeup of your class, you may decide to use three or four of your students' assessment methods per project or assignment.

4. Have students share their work and also the unique assessment methods they used to determine whether they learned the subject matter.

Discussion   1. Why is it important for teachers to assess student work in a variety of ways?

2. How would you prefer to have your knowledge represented?

3. How else can we make assignments more interesting?

Enrichment   Allow students the opportunity to assess your teaching.

Ask students a variety of questions to get their feedback on how to make the class—and their learning experience—more enjoyable.

ACTIVITY 5   Learning Options

Although learning can oftentimes be boring, it becomes exciting when what you are learning is relevant to your life and your interests. Unfortunately, students often report that they have no say about what they learn and that learning is too detached from their everyday lives.

Materials
▶ None

Instructions
1. Prior to embarking on a new unit of study, consider the following two questions: How does this unit relate to the everyday lives of my students? How are my students going to use this information in the future? If you can answer these two questions without hesitation, then you will be guaranteeing greater student engagement in the learning process.

2. Be creative in introducing the unit of study to your students. If, for example, you are introducing a lesson in chemistry focusing on the periodic table, take the time to help your students understand why and when this table is used. Let students ask questions without fear of embarrassment or teacher ridicule. Many students will sit through an entire lesson not really understanding what they are supposed to learn.

3. As a class, discuss the learning objectives of the unit and how the class is going to achieve those objectives.

Discussion
1. What makes a lesson or unit interesting?
2. What subjects do you find most relevant to your life?
3. What subjects do you find the most exciting? Why?

Enrichment
At the end of each unit of study, ask students to think about two questions that were not answered. The questions may concern aspects of the unit that were not discussed, or they may pertain to something the students simply did not understand. Questions should be submitted in writing so students feel they can ask anything without embarrassing themselves.

ACTIVITY 6   Fun with Paint

What kid doesn't like to get his or her hands messy with paint? By the time students get to high school, they rarely have the opportunity to get messy and just have fun. This finger-painting activity is sure to bring laughter and enjoyment to your classroom.

Materials   ► Finger paint and finger-paint paper

Instructions

1. Give each student several sheets of finger-paint paper and small amounts of finger paint.

2. Inform students that their next assignment will be to represent what they have learned by doing something they haven't done since they were youngsters—finger painting. Following are two examples of how to incorporate this activity in your classroom:

    If you recently finished a unit on the Civil War, have students paint something they learned about the war and some of the famous people who played an important part in the struggle. Their finished products will vary widely.

    If, in Spanish class, you taught students how to order food in a restaurant, have them show what they learned through finger painting. Some students may paint pictures of food, whereas others may paint pictures of restaurants or possibly the new words they used in class.

3. Allow students to share their works of art with the class.

Discussion

1. How did it feel to get your hands messy?

2. What was fun about this activity?

3. Can learning be fun? Why or why not?

Enrichment

Allow your students to express themselves through a variety of art projects. They may, for example, wish to use modeling clay when working on a project about the Civil War; a 3-D structure to solve a problem in math class; or a collage or mural to complete an English assignment.

Go Outside

Sometimes just getting a bit of fresh air can be fun and exciting. Sunlight, fresh air, and the opportunity to stretch can be invigorating for teachers as well as students. A change of routine—whether you go outside or simply use a different approach—is also a great way to infuse the condition of fun and excitement into the high school classroom.

Materials   ► None

Instructions

1. Give your students the opportunity to step outside the building for 5 minutes or so.

2. Assign students a task each time they go outside. For example, ask them to do any or all of the following: remain quiet and just listen, observe something they haven't paid close attention to before, shut their eyes and imagine they are anywhere else in the world. Consider this activity a short break during which students can relax mentally.

3. Ask students to think of other ways to refresh their minds during a 5-minute break.

Discussion

1. Why is it important to give our minds a break?

2. How do you relax outside of school?

3. What causes you the most stress at school?

Enrichment   Once a month, engage your students in a challenging physical activity that inspires them to be adventurous or challenges them to work together. Students will enjoy having fun and sharing laughter.

ACTIVITY 8   Scenarios for Fun and Excitement

Read the following scenarios to your students one at a time. After you have read each scenario, give students ample time to think about their responses to it and then engage them in a lively class discussion.

1. The student council has planned the same dance year after year. How can you help the students on the council broaden their scope so they can come up with different, more refreshing ideas?

2. Every year, your school plans sports pep rallies. The pep rallies are all alike, and within 10 minutes, most of the students are bored stiff. You are given the opportunity to plan the next student pep rally. What do you do?

3. The school is reexamining its homework policy. The administrators are concerned about the amount of homework that students are not completing. The students maintain that homework is boring and meaningless. You have been elected to represent the students. What policies would you implement to ensure that students view homework as meaningful? (Keep in mind that eliminating homework is not an option.)

Challenge Activities for Fun and Excitement

For Students   ▶ Allow your students to help develop and present fun and exciting lessons. You may be surprised at the wonderful insight the students have.

▶ Change your routine for a week. Instead of walking down the same hallway and saying hello to the same people, try taking a different route. Other twists: Eat lunch with someone new, do something different after school, or look into the possibility of joining a school-sponsored club or taking part in other extracurricular activities. By changing your routine, you will be bringing some spontaneity into your week.

▶ Let yourself be silly. Play games, watch cartoons, and just have fun.

For Teachers   ▶ Take the time to share a joke with your students. Let your hair down and just have fun for 5 minutes either before or after class.

▶ Be spontaneous with your students. Take them outside and have them look at the school building from a different perspective. Have them do stretching exercises. Ask them to dress differently than they normally would every day for a whole week. Keep them off guard, wondering why you are changing the class's routine.

▶ Bring some excitement into your staff meetings. Set aside some time to socialize. Help create fun and exciting ways to sift through all the mundane, boring information.

CHAPTER FIVE

CURIOSITY and CREATIVITY

CONFIDENCE to TAKE ACTION

LEADERSHIP and RESPONSIBILITY

SPIRIT of ADVENTURE

CURIOSITY and CREATIVITY

FUN and EXCITEMENT

SENSE of ACCOMPLISHMENT

HEROES

BELONGING

ACTIVITY 1   Who Am I?

By now, students have participated in a number of get-to-know-you activities. This activity requires students to be a bit creative and is a great way to start off a new class.

Materials
► A variety of common household items

Instructions
1. Inform your students that they are going to tell the class a little bit about themselves.
2. Have the students choose a common household item to help describe themselves.
3. In the front of the classroom, stock enough items (e.g., a fork, a pencil, a slip of paper, an apple) for each student in the class.
4. Have each student choose an item and then describe how this item represents or describes him or her. For example, students may choose a pencil because they are the scholarly type or perhaps because they are prone to making mistakes and like to correct them. They should not, however, choose an apple simply because they like to eat apples. Encourage students to be creative.
5. You may want to get the ball rolling at the start of the activity by selecting an item yourself. This will help the class understand the creative nature of the game.

Discussion
1. What is something new you learned about your classmates?
2. Was it difficult or easy to be creative? Why?
3. How can we be more creative in our everyday schoolwork?

Enrichment
Ask students to create a collage of symbols or pictures that represent them. The only catch is that the pictures cannot be obvious. For example, if students like to play soccer, they cannot include soccer balls in the collage. Instead, they might choose black-and-white items (the same color as soccer balls), the color green (to indicate the grass soccer field), and something that makes noise (to represent a whistle). This is a great activity to get the creative juices flowing.

ACTIVITY 2   Learning Styles

Understanding how one learns is a key component of success at school and at work. For example, some people like to read, whereas others prefer to have someone else read to them. In order to help students understand the learning process, it is important for them to be aware of their individual learning styles and needs.

Materials   ▶ Learning Styles Worksheet

Instructions   1. Encourage your students to think about learning—to think about what their favorite subjects are and why.

2. Give students the Learning Styles Worksheet. Tell them not to mark on it until you have given them the OK, but do have them read the instructions at the top.

3. Read to your students the following: *The statements on the worksheet represent the different ways we learn. How do you like to learn?*

4. Have students rate each statement. (Depending on how much time you wish to spend on this activity, you may want to add questions to the worksheet.)

5. Have students look over their responses and ask them what those responses say about them as learners.

Discussion   1. What types of assignments work best for you as learners?

2. What assignments are the most difficult for you? Why?

3. How can teachers better understand you as a learner?

Enrichment   Explore multiple intelligences with your students. Have students help create lessons and assessment methods for all intelligences.

Learning Styles Worksheet

Read the following statements about learning styles and rate them on a scale of 1 to 5.
If you very much like the style of learning indicated by the statement, rate it a 1.
If you like it somewhat, rate it a 2.
If you feel neutral about it, rate it a 3.
If you dislike it somewhat, rate it a 4.
If you dislike it a great deal, rate it a 5.

1. I like to read. _____

2. I like to listen to lectures. _____

3. I like to work with my hands. _____

4. I like to interact with people. _____

5. I like to work alone. _____

6. I like to discover answers on my own. _____

7. I like to have someone give me the answers. _____

8. I like to keep a pencil in my hand. _____

9. I like to use a dictionary. _____

10. I like to walk around occasionally. _____

ACTIVITY 3　　　Interpreting Art

Using art is probably the best way to help students explore their creative side. Unfortunately, by the time students reach high school, they often have already decided whether or not they are artistic. Still, it is important to allow all students to express themselves through art. This is a fun and engaging activity that will bring out the budding artist in all students. In it, students are asked to create an abstract drawing or painting, share it with the class, and then explain the deeper meaning of their classmates' artwork.

Materials　▶ Art supplies

Instructions　1. Give students drawing paper, paint, markers, crayons, and other art materials and instruct them to create an abstract picture.

2. After you have given students enough time to create, collect their masterpieces and distribute them randomly to their classmates.

3. As the students look at each other's work, have them explain the picture they have been given. (First, you may want to demonstrate to the class how one can creatively explain a picture.)

4. After a student explains another's picture, have the artist of that picture explain what he or she was thinking about when creating it. Continue until everyone has had a chance to share.

Discussion　1. What does it feel like to express yourself through artwork?

2. Who decides what is or is not art?

3. Other than through drawing, how else can we creatively represent ourselves?

Enrichment　Collect a variety of work by famous artists or photographers (e.g., the artists Monet and Picasso, the famous Civil War photographer Mathew Brady). Make sure to choose work that can be interpreted in myriad ways, and ask your students for their interpretations: What was the artist trying to depict? After the class has shared their ideas, provide them with a few interpretations offered by professional artists. Whose interpretations are correct?

ACTIVITY 4   World Issues

Throughout history, people who think creatively have developed wonderful inventions and devised solutions to world problems. Although all jobs require some form of creativity, it is curiosity that will always spur people on to achieve at higher levels. This activity challenges students to look at issues in different ways.

Materials   ▶ Writing paper and pencils or pens

Instructions   1. Either ahead of time or together with your students, choose a global topic such as hunger, pollution, or civil war.

2. After you have decided on an issue, ask your students to think about all the solutions to the problem that they have heard about and write them on a piece of paper.

3. Collect the papers and read the solutions to the class.

4. Divide the class into groups of three and then inform the students that they are going to be given time to develop their own solutions to the issues they chose. Tell them that they may not, however, choose the solutions that you have read aloud and that they must think of unique and creative solutions.

5. After you have given the groups enough time to think about their solutions, allow them to share their solutions with the other groups in the class.

Discussion   1. Why was it so difficult to think of unique solutions?

2. Why do we often seem to look for the same solutions to old problems?

3. What are some other problems that you think could use a fresh perspective?

Enrichment   Use this same technique to look at school issues or problems. What creative solutions can the students develop for these problems? Give the students an opportunity to present their solutions to those in the school who are trying to deal with the problems.

ACTIVITY 5   Extemporaneous Speeches

It is often difficult to be creative when one is unprepared for the task at hand and is also facing the pressure of time constraints. This is a fun activity that forces students to be creative and literally think on their feet. Even students who are shy and don't enjoy being in front of crowds have fun with this activity.

Materials
► Enough slips of paper for everyone in the class
► A hat

Instructions
1. Prior to the activity, write various funny speech titles on the slips of paper and put them in the hat. You may use silly titles such as "Red All Over" or "My, the Sky Is Blue" or "Messy Spaghetti."
2. Inform students that they are going to draw a slip of paper from the hat and then give a 1-minute speech relating to the title they have chosen.
3. As the students get better at this activity and begin to feel more confident, think of additional titles that will make it more difficult for them to be creative in their speech making.

Discussion
1. What was challenging about this activity?
2. When else have you been in a situation where you had to think on your feet?
3. Why is speaking in front of crowds easy for some people and difficult for others?

Enrichment
This same activity can be done using sounds. In secret, give students a sound that they must describe without making that particular noise or saying the word. One example might be the sound of a car horn. Have them give a 1-minute speech and see if the class can guess what sound they are describing.

ACTIVITY 6   How Does It Work?

Even the smartest people have difficulty understanding how certain things work. Many students listen to CDs every day, yet how many of them really know how they work? Even the workings of something as common as a car engine are a mystery to many students and adults.

Materials
- ▶ Access to the school library

Instructions

1. Ask students to think about inventions: What inventions are perplexing to them? What inventions do they admire the most?

2. Have the class choose an invention or device whose mechanism they would like to understand better. The item should be something that the class can see and touch (e.g., a CD or a TV remote control).

3. Ask the students to put their heads together and try to figure out how the device works. If the class is large, you may want students to split up into smaller groups, with each group responsible for focusing on a different feature of the device. You may even decide to divide the class in half and have each half figure out the workings of a different item or invention.

4. Once the students have researched their project, allow them plenty of time to present their findings.

Discussion

1. What do you think is the most surprising invention of all time?

2. What invention do you think changed the course of history the most?

3. If you could invent a cure for one disease, what would it be?

Enrichment

Have your students create an infomercial for a new product. Tell them they must develop the product, write the script for the infomercial, and then present the infomercial to the class. Tell them also that they must be able to create a mock-up of the item.

ACTIVITY 7   Standout College Essays

Many high school students face what they consider an arduous task—writing entrance essays for colleges they wish to attend. They may not realize, however, that those at the college who are responsible for reading their essays may face an even more strenuous task— reading thousands of essays that, for the most part, all sound alike. This activity challenges your students to write creative and dynamic college essays.

Materials
- ► Sample applications from a variety of colleges and universities (available on-line)
- ► A number of essay questions from the same schools (available on-line)

Instructions
1. Select a number of college essay questions and distribute them randomly to your students. Have the class write their essays, but challenge them to be as creative as possible so that each of theirs stands out among the thousands of essays that will be read by the readers in the college admissions office.
2. Help students as they think about how they can be creative in their writing. As a class, brainstorm what it means to be creative.
3. Allow students sufficient time to write their essays and encourage them to share the essays with the class.

Discussion
1. Why is it difficult to write creatively?
2. What do you think essay readers look for in a good essay?
3. What question would you ask on a college application?

Enrichment
Take this activity one step further by conducting mock college interviews with your students.

Prepare a list of questions and have students use them as they interview each other.

Read the following scenarios to your students one at a time. After you have read each scenario, give students ample time to think about their responses to it and then engage them in a lively class discussion.

1. In one of your classes you have been told that assignments, essays, and test questions all have have only one correct answer. You disagree. Make your case.

2. You notice that a new car model is being unveiled this week. The car is supposed to be the best on the market. In your opinion, what features would that car need to make it truly new, exciting, and dynamic? (Be creative and remember that the sky is the limit.)

3. Explore your creative side: Your school is reconfiguring its student council. How would you re-create your student council to make it more meaningful to and representative of the student body?

Challenge Activities for Curiosity and Creativity

For Students
- ► Challenge students to ask "why" and "why not" questions in their classes and when they are with their friends. Ask them if there is any reason they should not try harder and do better?
- ► Challenge students not to take the easy way out whenever they have a choice of assignments. Encourage them to be creative and to try something a bit different.
- ► Challenge students to use photography or artwork as they undertake their next assignment.

For Teachers
- ► Teach a lesson that is new and interesting to you. Surprise your students with an unexpected lesson on a subject that intrigues them.
- ► Create multiple assessment opportunities for your students. Allow students the opportunity to choose their assessment.
- ► Integrate music and fine arts into your lessons and curriculum.

CHAPTER SIX

SPIRIT of ADVENTURE

CONFIDENCE to TAKE ACTION

LEADERSHIP and RESPONSIBILITY

SPIRIT of ADVENTURE

CURIOSITY and CREATIVITY

FUN and EXCITEMENT

SENSE of ACCOMPLISHMENT

HEROES

BELONGING

ACTIVITY 1   **Looking Different**

In every high school, many students have a tendency to stick together in various cliques. Some of these cliques pride themselves on dressing the same, whereas others place an emphasis on wearing the same hairstyle or walking and talking a certain way. It is easy to see that, for many students, it is a huge risk not to conform. After all, students do not want to be considered outcasts.

Materials ▶ None

Instructions
1. Discuss with your students why it is that people dress the way they do. Ask them questions such as the following:

   Why do you dress like your friends?

   Why do you and your friends have similar haircuts and take part in the same activities?

   What phrases do you and your friends commonly use?

2. Challenge your students not to follow the group for a day. This challenge may require them to dress differently, do something unique with their hair, or just hang out with other people.

3. Let students know that you realize how difficult this task will be, but tell them you want to challenge them.

Discussion
1. Why was it difficult not to follow the group?
2. What was one positive result of your experience?
3. Do you think it is important to take healthy risks? Explain.

Enrichment   Together with your students, research stories of those who took risks in order to make a difference for a group of people. These risk takers may include people who stood up against oppression or questioned some of their government's policies. What happened to those individuals who were not successful in their efforts?

My Zones

The condition of spirit of adventure is about healthy risk taking. The important thing to remember about this condition is that it is unique to the individual. For example, one student may consider it a huge risk to give a class presentation, whereas another student may find it easy to speak in front of the class. The challenge for teachers is to understand each student's tolerance for risk and then help all students better understand themselves.

Materials
► My Zones Worksheet
► Pencils or pens
► Chart paper, tape, and markers

Instructions
1. Introduce your students to the three zones of the condition of spirit of adventure.

   The first zone is the *comfort zone*. While in this zone, people feel very comfortable. For many of them, tasks and activities that fall under this category include reading, watching TV, or playing sports. People do not feel anxious while in this zone and find it easy to accomplish whatever activity they are engaged in.

   The second zone is the *challenge zone*. While in this zone, people feel somewhat challenged. The activities that people in this zone engage in may include, for example, taking up a new sport or speaking to a large audience. Although these people will notice that they feel a bit anxious, they still find that they are capable of accomplishing these tasks. To achieve success in this zone is quite rewarding.

   The third zone is the *panic zone*. While in this zone, people feel virtually helpless because they are confronted with a task for which they are unprepared or haven't the experience. They know they have little chance of succeeding, and the mere thought of the activity brings on panic. Pushing people into their panic zone will thwart future risk-taking efforts.

2. Give students the My Zones Worksheet and have them write down a few activities under each category of zones. You, too, should follow suit, as well as prompt students by representing the zones visually through drawings or words on the chalkboard.

3. Tape three pieces of chart paper on a wall, with each piece of paper representing one of the three zones.

4. Ask students to transfer the activities they wrote on their worksheet to the appropriate piece of chart paper on the wall. You will quickly see that one student's comfort zone is another student's challenge or panic zone. Ask students to discuss their observations.

5. Lead the class in a discussion about risk taking and moving beyond one's comfort zone. Use your own personal examples and discuss the rewards that occur when you master a task.

Discussion
1. What surprised you about your classmates' zones?
2. How can you move from one zone to the next?
3. Which zone do you spend most of your time in? Explain.

Enrichment
Have your students keep a journal of their zones for an entire week, listing under the appropriate category their activities each day. By keeping a journal, your students will be able to self-assess their risk-taking behavior.

My Zones Worksheet

Comfort Zone	Challenge Zone	Panic Zone

Raising Student Aspirations: Classroom Activities for Grades 9–12
© 2003 by Russell J. Quaglia and Kristine M. Fox. Champaign, IL: Research Press (800) 519-2707

Have You Ever?

Although risk taking is often associated with daredevil stunts and extreme sports, danger is not a necessary ingredient. The truth is, many ways exist for people to take risks that are healthy and that also celebrate the condition of spirit of adventure. Healthy risk taking should be encouraged and acknowledged in schools every day. This activity is a fun way for students to learn about their classmates' spirit of adventure.

Materials
► A slip of paper for each student
► Pencils or pens

Instructions
1. Distribute the slips of paper to the class and ask them to list three experiences: (a) something they have done that they never thought they would do, such as running a marathon or eating sushi; (b) something they would like to do but are afraid to do, such as skydiving or taking a class in calculus; and (c) something they have not done, but something that their classmates may or may not think they have done (i.e., a fabrication).

2. One by one, have students read aloud to the class—in random order—the three items on their list.

3. After each student has read the three items, have the rest of the class try to guess (a) which activity they think the student has actually engaged in; (b) which activity they think the student would like to engage in but hasn't; and (c) which activity the student listed merely as a fabrication.

4. Ask the class to decide who among them is the biggest *healthy* risk taker. Ask them to think about the following: What personality traits allow this person to be a big risk taker? How can we all become better and healthier risk takers?

Discussion
1. Do you consider yourself a risk taker? Why or why not?
2. Outside of this class, whom do you consider to be a risk taker? Explain.
3. What academic risks are you willing to take this year?

Enrichment
Ask each student to pick two healthy school risks. The risks may range from joining a school club to taking an advanced course. Students should share their progress, as well as their setbacks, throughout the year.

ACTIVITY 4   **Animal Risk Takers**

There are many different kinds of risk takers. Some people look before they leap, whereas others leap before they look. There is no one right way to be a healthy risk taker. After engaging students in a brief discussion of risk taking, challenge them to take part in this activity.

Materials   ▶ Drawing paper and markers

Instructions   1. Ask students to draw an animal that represents who they are as a risk taker.

2. Have the students turn the paper over and draw the animal that they would prefer to have represent them as a risk taker.

3. Ask students to explain their drawings to the class.

Discussion   1. Why do we vary so widely when it comes to risk taking?

2. Can you be successful without also being a risk taker?

3. When is it bad to be a risk taker?

Enrichment   Ask students to write fables about the animals they have drawn. Each fable should include a lesson about risk taking.

ACTIVITY 5   Add Some Spice

This activity, which introduces students to different spices, is a fun way to promote the condition of spirit of adventure. A good way to pique students' interest is to tell them they are going to go on a tasting expedition.

Materials
- ► A variety of spices
- ► Samples of food prepared with those spices
- ► Small paper cups
- ► Markers

Instructions
1. Sprinkle various spices in the paper cups and then number the cups for future identification.
2. Tell the class that you would like their opinion of certain spices.
3. Ask for volunteers (risk takers) who are willing to try a small sample of a spice. Make sure you solicit two or more tasters per cup.
4. After the volunteers have sampled the spices, ask them how the spices looked, smelled, and tasted.
5. Tell the class what spice is in each numbered cup.
6. As a reward for the risk takers, serve them samples of food prepared with some of the spices on display. If, for example, ginger was one of the spices used, give the volunteer a ginger snap cookie. If one of the spices was anise, give the volunteer a piece of licorice, which has an anise taste.

Discussion
1. Why are some students willing to be tasters and others are not?
2. Is it difficult to be a risk taker when you are faced with the unknown? Explain.
3. What exotic foods have you tried?

Enrichment   Ask each student to prepare a dish made with a mystery ingredient. There must, however, be enough of the ingredient in the dish to make it stand out. For example, a flake of Italian seasoning in a chocolate chip cookie would not count.

Heads Up!

Allowing students to have fun, be themselves, and work together is a great way to build risk-taking skills. Students who are risk takers are confident and find that people tend to support their initiatives. As students begin to understand each other better, the more supportive they are apt to be. Unfortunately, some students find it risky to have fun and be silly.

Materials   ▶ Small beanbags or sandwich bags filled with beans

Instructions   1. Divide the class into two groups, or teams, and have them move to opposite ends of the classroom.

2. Have students put a beanbag on top of their heads and instruct them to keep their hands at their sides.

3. Tell students the game is played as follows:

> The object is to walk across the room without having your beanbag fall off your head.

> If the bag falls off your head, you must stop and wait for a teammate to rescue you.

> In order to rescue you, the teammate must pick up your beanbag and place it back on your head without losing his or her own beanbag.

> If your rescuer's bag falls off in the process, he or she must also stop, which means both of you now need to be rescued.

> If you have successfully crossed the finish line (i.e., with beanbag intact), you cannot try to rescue a teammate unless you go back to the starting line and begin anew.

> The first team to get all its members across the finish line is the winner.

Discussion   1. What did it feel like to do this activity? Why is it a risk to be silly?

2. How did you have to work as a team to be successful?

3. What got in the way of your being a successful risk taker during this activity?

Enrichment   Once a month, ask a pair of students to introduce a silly activity for the class to try.

ACTIVITY 7   Choose Your Own Grade

Although most high school students have been introduced to the concept of goal setting, it is rarely reinforced with much consistency. The condition of spirit of adventure promotes goal setting as a way to act in the present to reach a goal. We have found that, although many students have wonderful dreams, they often do little or nothing in the present to help themselves realize their dreams. This activity adds a twist to the teaching of goal setting. It encourages students to choose between several different goals before they start learning a unit, and it works well for any subject.

Materials   ▶ None

Instructions   1. Prior to beginning a unit of study, tell your students what they need to accomplish to receive a particular grade—A, A-, B+, B, and so on. Some teachers develop rubrics for each unit. Once they do, students can then choose what grade they wish to obtain.

2. Obviously, to achieve an A, students will be required to put in a good deal more time and effort than those students who do not choose to set that high a goal. Students who choose the higher grades as their goals should be supported in their endeavors. All grades should have a self-assessment component as a requirement.

3. After you have completed this activity, allow time to get together with each student individually and discuss the results. It is hoped that students who choose to achieve lower grades will come to realize that, with a bit of effort, they, too, can achieve at a higher level.

Discussion   1. Why is it important for students to decide on their own the grade they wish to achieve?

2. Why are some students afraid of success?

3. If you did not reach your goal, what can you do differently next time to improve?

Enrichment   Allow students to help develop tests for the class. Have students develop several tests and then choose bits and pieces from each test to produce one major exam.

Scenarios for Spirit of Adventure

Read the following scenarios to your students one at a time. After you have read each scenario, give students ample time to think about their responses to it and then engage them in a lively class discussion.

1. From the time they begin school, students are told that it is all right to fail, as long as they try their best. There are students who adhere to this notion, and, as a result, failure means nothing to them. In fact, they are more afraid of success than failure. Explain.

2. Although your friends seem willing to do and try anything, you are almost always afraid to follow suit. They speak their minds, exude confidence, and make their own decisions. You want to be more like them, but you can't seem to get up the courage to take risks. How can you help yourself become a better risk taker?

3. Your music class requires you to sing a solo in order to pass the class. You are petrified of this assignment because you think you may be tone deaf. Your teacher insists that everyone can learn to sing. How do you address this issue and prepare yourself for the assignment?

4. Your best friend is constantly taking foolish risks. If someone dares her to do something wild, she will almost always do it; she thinks it is fun and exciting. You are concerned for her safety. What can you do?

Challenge Activities for Spirit of Adventure

For Students
- Challenge students to set goals and to follow through until they achieve them. Have them start a goal journal at home and keep track of their progress.

- Encourage students to accept a challenging assignment. This assignment may involve doing something that is a bit intimidating or that requires a bit of extra work.

- Challenge students not to spend an entire day in their comfort zone. Have them challenge themselves academically, athletically, socially, musically, or any other healthy way you or they can think of.

For Teachers
- Take the time to understand your own comfort, challenge, and panic zones. What can you do to challenge yourself professionally? Go out on a limb and try something new.

- Get involved with your school's goals and vision of the future. Are they meaningful? Does the school operate in a way that exemplifies its goals and vision? What does the school need to do differently to meet its stated goals and vision of the future?

- Change your routines for a week. If you usually walk into the teacher's room when you enter the school, try hanging out in the hallways. If you normally spend lunch period in your room, try eating with colleagues for a week. Changing your routines can be a great way to model the condition of spirit of adventure.

CHAPTER SEVEN

LEADERSHIP and RESPONSIBILITY

CONFIDENCE to TAKE ACTION

LEADERSHIP and RESPONSIBILITY

SPIRIT of ADVENTURE

CURIOSITY and CREATIVITY

FUN and EXCITEMENT

SENSE of ACCOMPLISHMENT

HEROES

BELONGING

ACTIVITY 1   Success Together

Although being a leader can often be a lonely job, it can also help make for a wonderful group experience. Those with leadership skills motivate groups to complete projects successfully so they can then enjoy the fruits of their labor. This activity encourages students to work together to achieve success. It can be worked into your curriculum and also applied across subjects.

Materials
- ▶ 6 index cards
- ▶ Writing paper and pencils or pens

Instructions

1. Ask your class to plan and implement a school event. The event should be geared toward parents, younger students, senior citizens in the community, or some other group—not their fellow high school students.

2. Create and hand out leadership cards. These cards are easy to prepare. Simply take six index cards and jot down one of the following leadership roles on each: leader, leader's helper, note taker, task keeper, summarizer (of who is to do what), and questioner (the one who asks questions to ensure that every contingency has been provided for).

3. Prior to each student planning session, distribute the leadership cards randomly, but make a point of redistributing them from time to time during the planning phase so that every student has a chance to assume some type of leadership role.

4. Make sure that students cover all the bases. For example, if they are planning a game night for elementary students or a dance for senior citizens, see that they have gotten permission from the administration to hold the event, that they have contacted those outside the school who need to be notified, and that they have done their planning properly so they are able to procure the necessary supplies and decorations.

5. If this project is too big an undertaking, try using leadership cards for a small class project. Perhaps the class is participating in a science fair or math meet. Using leadership cards allows students who usually don't take on leadership roles the opportunity to practice and test their leadership skills.

Discussion

1. How difficult was it to follow directions and carry out your assignments?

2. Which role did you like the best?

3. What is it like trying to make group decisions?

Enrichment

Once a month, create a class project that requires students to figure out a way to work together in order to be successful. The projects do not have to be big—just challenging.

Decision Making

Making important decisions when faced with an assortment of choices is difficult for people of all ages. When students are younger, they have to make only minor decisions, such as what toy they want for their birthday. As they enter middle school, they are challenged to make decisions involving peer pressure (i.e., whether to follow the crowd). By the time they reach high school, many students have established their identity and must now use that identity as a basis for making any number of decisions (e.g., Does the tough guy have to fight? Do the wild kids have to do dangerous things?). This activity encourages students to make decisions and think about the consequences of their decisions. In the process, it helps to promote the condition of leadership and responsibility.

Materials ▸ Scholarship Candidates' Biographies

Instructions

1. Divide the class into groups of five and give each group the Scholarship Candidates' Biographies.

2. After the groups have decided who should receive the scholarship, bring the class together to share their decision-making experiences. Have them defend their choice of candidates and then question that choice and make a case for another candidate whenever possible.

Discussion

1. How did your group come to a group decision? What process did you use?

2. As a group, how do you arrive at a compromise on difficult decisions?

3. What compromises have you been asked to make in a decision-making situation?

Enrichment Obtain the records of a court case. Allow students to read both sides of the case—the plaintiff's and the defendant's. Divide students into small groups and ask them to serve as jurors. What did they decide and why? You may want to choose a historically significant court case for the students to consider.

Scholarship Candidates' Biographies

Your group has been chosen to award one college scholarship. It is a four-year scholarship, and it is to be awarded to one of the following six candidates, each of whom qualifies to attend college. You must decide who the most deserving candidate is by considering how the student, the school, and society as a whole will benefit from his or her receiving the scholarship.

Keep in mind that everyone in your group must agree with the decision. If you cannot reach a unanimous decision, then none of the candidates will be awarded the scholarship. Here are brief biographies of the candidates:

Sarah

Sarah will be the first student in her family to attend college. She has worked really hard at school and helps support her family with a nighttime job. She really wants to go to college but does not know how she will be able to afford it. Sarah wants to study to be a teacher.

John

John was a bit of a slacker in high school. He did not study much or care a lot about school. John did great on his SAT and is obviously bright. He says that, if he receives the scholarship, he will go to school and try hard. If he does not get the scholarship, John is likely to end up with the wrong crowd and run into trouble with the law.

Jacob

Jacob is well liked by everyone. He did well in high school and wants to go to college and study to be a doctor. He aspires to find a cure for cancer. Jacob has cancer himself, and his doctors are unsure of his prognosis.

Catrina

Catrina comes from a college-educated family. It was always expected that she would go to school and follow in the footsteps of her parents and grandparents. Catrina is an average student, but she desires to go to college. Catrina thought paying for tuition was not going to be an issue. However, her parents have informed her that their business is bankrupt and they cannot help pay for her college tuition.

Zachary

Zachary's father died when he was a youngster. He has struggled with the death of his father and has had a difficult time making friends. Zachary's mother has not been around much, but she does want her son to go to college. Zachary is involved in a serious relationship with his girlfriend, who is a waitress and does not want Zachary to go to college. Zachary would like to study political science.

Kate

Kate uses a wheelchair and has difficulty writing. She managed, however, to be in the very top of her graduating class. Kate would like to be an advocate for people with disabilities.

ACTIVITY 3   Leadership Myths

Although the concept of leadership sounds easy, it is actually multi-faceted. Ask a group of students or adults to define leadership and they will struggle with the answer; no two definitions of leadership will be the same. This activity asks students to explore some common leadership myths.

Materials ▶ List of Leadership Traits

Instructions 1. Divide the class into groups of four and give each group the List of Leadership Traits.

2. Instruct the groups to discuss the statements, agree or disagree with the statements, and then defend their points of view.

3. After discussing the groups' views, inform the class that the four statements are not necessarily true. Explain that they are really myths—assumptions about leaders and leadership that sometimes are true and sometimes are false. Explain why these statements are overgeneralizations that are not necessarily true:

> Statement No. 1: Leadership skills actually can be taught. There are plenty of examples of people who did not become leaders until late in life.

> Statement No. 2: Leaders can in fact be either introverted or extroverted. They can have just about any personality traits.

> Statement No. 3: Just because someone holds a position of authority does not necessarily mean that he or she is a leader. In many instances, the true student leader is not the president of the student council but rather some other person who is trusted and respected by the rest of the students.

> Statement No. 4: Actually, some leaders lead and guide their followers to make decisions. Clearly, decision making is important, but leaders are not always the ones who make the decisions.

4. Give students time to discuss these myths. Ask them to think about other leadership myths and share them with the class.

Discussion 1. What makes people follow negative leaders or leaders of cults?

2. What one trait do you look for in a leader?

3. What leadership trait would you most like to develop?

Enrichment Ask students to create the perfect leader. What traits would this leader possess? How would this leader work with his or her followers? What positions would he or she stand for and advocate?

List of Leadership Traits

Statement 1:

Leaders are born, not made.

Statement 2:

In order to be a leader, you must be an extrovert.

Statement 3:

Leaders hold positions of authority.

Statement 4:

Leaders make decisions.

Raising Student Aspirations: Classroom Activities for Grades 9–12
© 2003 by Russell J. Quaglia and Kristine M. Fox. Champaign, IL: Research Press (800) 519-2707

ACTIVITY 4   Teach the Class

Allowing students the opportunity to teach others is a wonderful way to imbue them with an important leadership skill. This activity is a fun way to teach this particular skill and at the same time let students practice their speaking and presentation skills.

Materials
- Enough How-To Cards for the entire class
- Optional: note paper and pencils or pens

Instructions
1. Turn the How-To Cards facedown, spread them out on a table or desk, and have each student choose one.
2. Give students ample time to plan a presentation, and then have them teach the skill written on their How-To Card to the rest of the class.
3. This activity can also be done in conjunction with a particular unit of study. For example, if the class is reading a book about 18th-century England, you might want to create How-To Cards that are specific to the book or the time period or both. Regardless, keep in mind that the main objective of this activity is for students to teach and not merely to write a paper or prepare a list of ideas.

Discussion
1. What was the most difficult part about teaching?
2. What does a good presenter do to interest the audience?
3. What subject would you like to teach?

Enrichment
Give as many students as possible the opportunity to co-teach a lesson with you. Have students help with planning and assessing the lesson.

How-To Cards

How to bake chocolate chip cookies	**How to play soccer**	**How to build a tree house**
How to play checkers	**How to play basketball**	**How to play baseball**
How to play pinochle	**How to build a paper airplane**	**How to play volleyball**
How to grow tomatoes	**How to write a poem**	**How to grill a hamburger**
How to build a campfire	**How to do the breaststroke**	**How to give a speech**
How to _____	**How to** _____	**How to** _____
How to _____	**How to** _____	**How to** _____
How to _____	**How to** _____	**How to** _____

ACTIVITY 5   Debating

Strong debating skills are important and beneficial for students to develop. Unfortunately, debating is not a skill that is readily taught in high school. This activity encourages students to debate an issue, even though they may have to take a stance that they personally oppose.

Materials
► A list of controversial topics important to your students

Instructions
1. Divide the class into groups of eight and assign each group a controversial topic to debate. Make sure you assign these topics randomly. Inform students that half their group must argue in support of the statement or topic they are given, whereas the other half must argue against it.

2. Prior to the debate, clarify a few rules with the students:

   Each group will be allotted a specified amount of time to make their points.

   Each side will be allowed two rebuttals.

   Points should be factual and not entirely emotional.

3. Once the groups have had enough time to prepare their debate, have one debating group come to the front of the room. Let the debate begin.

4. Students who are watching the debate should decide which side is more convincing.

Discussion
1. What was difficult about debating?
2. How do you settle disagreements with your friends?
3. Why is the ability to debate a good leadership skill to have?

Enrichment
Give your students the opportunity to visit a courtroom and watch lawyers present their cases. Students will be fascinated by this process.

Let your students watch congressional or parliamentary debates on TV. Be sure to allow time for discussion.

ACTIVITY 6   Straw Houses

Good leaders have the ability to plan and implement their ideas. This activity is a fun way to encourage students to be good planners.

Materials
- Drinking straws
- Tape
- Scissors
- Paper clips
- Hole punches

Instructions

1. Let students know that they are going to be challenged to build a straw house and that each of them will be supplied with the same amount of materials.
2. Inform students that their house must be at least a foot tall and that they will be given 3 minutes to plan their house.
3. Tell students they now have 15 minutes to build their house.
4. After they have built their house, tell students that they must watch as three of their classmates try to blow their house over within 20 seconds. The three students can neither touch the house nor disturb the desk or table on which the house has been built.
5. Have fun with this activity and poll the class to see who they think is the best planner.

Discussion

1. Would you rather plan a project or jump right in with both feet? Explain.
2. Have you every planned a project and then had to change everything? Explain.
3. Has there ever been a time when you did not plan but should have? Explain.

Enrichment

Ask an architect to visit your class and share his or her plans for a project as well as pictures of the final product.

Student Surveys

It is important for leaders to know what their followers want. The ability to develop survey and research techniques is a wonderful skill for students to have. This activity encourages students to create, administer, and analyze a survey.

Materials
- ▶ Information about the development of surveys
- ▶ Sample surveys
- ▶ Personal computers that students can use to create surveys

Instructions
1. Begin this activity by distributing examples of surveys to your students. The surveys might be from restaurants, auto clubs, grocery stores, or other businesses or organizations. Further engage students by asking them about surveys they may have responded to in the past.

2. Tell students that they are going to develop a survey. First, have them think about a population or segment of society they want to survey, such as their own community, their school, teachers, or police. Next, have them think about what they want to learn or discover from their survey.

3. Provide students with a brief introduction to survey development. For the purposes of this activity, survey questions should not be open-ended.

4. Give students enough time to develop their surveys, ensuring that they have access to a personal computer for compiling their survey questions.

5. After students have created their surveys, let them administer the surveys. This part of the activity will take some time, depending on the population the students are surveying. Be sure to give students enough time—possibly a week or so—to administer their surveys.

6. Once their surveys have been administered, have students tabulate the results and share their findings with the class. Encourage students to plan and give a presentation that might include graphs and other visual aids.

7. Make sure the students share their survey results with the people they surveyed.

Discussion
1. What did you learn about the population you surveyed?
2. Why are surveys a good way to gather information?
3. What constitutes a good survey?

Enrichment
Coordinate a survey activity with the math teacher, introducing the students to some basic concepts pertaining both to the gathering of statistics and to statistical analysis.

Encourage students to read books or articles that discuss how it is possible for statistics to be manipulated in such a way that they do not accurately reflect what it is that the survey was intended to measure.

Ask your students to find and share examples of poor surveys, inferior survey techniques, and exaggerated conclusions.

ACTIVITY 8   Scenarios for Leadership and Responsibility

Read the following scenarios to your students one at a time. After you have read each scenario, give students ample time to think about their responses to it and then engage them in a lively class discussion.

1. You have been designated the leader of your group of friends. You did not ask to be the leader, but everyone looks to you whenever it comes time to decide the group's next move. Someone in your group is getting involved with issues that could get him in trouble. As a leader, what do you do?

2. Your school's student council is a waste of time. The popular kids are always elected, and they never do anything. Being on the student council is just an excuse to get out of class and a way to spice up your college applications. You truly want the opportunity to be a leader. How do you change the student council to make it a true leadership group?

3. Your school has decided to cut its after-school programs. Obviously, this development is upsetting to most students. How do you go about doing something to ensure that students' ideas and opinions are heard by the administration?

Challenge Activities for Leadership and Responsibility

For Students
- ► Challenge students to join a decision-making group so that they can voice their opinions on certain issues.
- ► Encourage students to challenge a decision that has been made by a teacher, administrator, or student leader that they do not agree with. Make sure you have enough information and facts to support your ideas and opinions.
- ► Challenge students to take the time to listen to the other side of an argument or debate. Encourage them to keep an open mind and face the reality that other people's opinions are as valid as their own.

For Teachers
- ► Allow your students to make more classroom decisions. Greater student input will bring more meaning and purpose to their studies.
- ► Be part of a decision-making group at your school. Make sure your voice is heard.
- ► Make a point to attend school board and PTA meetings. Let these groups know what you are thinking.

CHAPTER EIGHT

CONFIDENCE to TAKE ACTION

CONFIDENCE to TAKE ACTION

LEADERSHIP and RESPONSIBILITY

SPIRIT of ADVENTURE

CURIOSITY and CREATIVITY

FUN and EXCITEMENT

SENSE of ACCOMPLISHMENT

HEROES

BELONGING

ACTIVITY 1   Survival Kit for New Students

Enrolling at a new school is difficult for any high school student. It is especially difficult for students who lack confidence in their classroom abilities or social skills. This activity forces students who are not new to their school to put themselves in the place of a new student.

Materials ► Items that each student decides to include in his or her Survival Kit for New Students

Instructions 1. Ask everyone in the class to create a Survival Kit for New Students. The kit should contain items that will be helpful to someone new to the school. Encourage students to be creative in developing their kits.

2. After students have put together their kits, they should write notes explaining the purpose of each item.

3. Ask students to share their kits with their classmates.

Discussion 1. What would it be like for a new student coming to this school?

2. How does someone make friends at this age?

3. What is the most important thing for new students to know about this school?

Enrichment Encourage each student to create a handbook for new students. The handbook might include humorous stories written in the school vernacular, but it should also be composed of practical information that would be helpful to a new student. For example, it might offer tips on how to become involved in sports, where to go with questions about courses, or what foods to steer clear of in the cafeteria.

Act It Out

Building students' confidence is as important in high school as it is in elementary and middle school—perhaps even more important as students approach graduation. This activity is fun in that it helps to build students' confidence in a lighthearted way.

Materials
► Napkins

Instructions
1. Inform students that you are going to ask them to go out on a limb and risk being laughed at. The laughter, however, will all be in fun.

2. Give students a napkin. Then ask them to use the napkin to describe a variety of scenarios and characteristics, such as the following:

   Their relationship with their best friend

   Their greatest asset

   Their worst fault

   Their plans for the future

   Their feelings come graduation day

3. Students should catch on quickly and enjoy this alternative way of looking at and describing their goals and dreams.

Discussion
1. If you had to create an award for yourself, what would it be named?

2. If given the opportunity, what color would you choose for your napkin and why?

3. What is a napkin metaphor you could use that relates to your hopes and dreams?

Enrichment
Ask each student to create a dream book. This book should list and explain the things the student hopes to accomplish sometime in the future. Each dream book should be strictly personal and give the student a chance to express his or her thoughts and ideas without anyone else knowing about them.

ACTIVITY 3   Make a Change

Students frequently talk about changes they would like to see made at school. Sometimes it's a class or a project that they don't like; other times it's social events that they think could be improved. This activity challenges students to think through their ideas and make plans to change what they don't like.

Materials
- ▶ Loose-leaf writing paper and pencils or pens
- ▶ A loose-leaf binder

Instructions
1. Tell students they have been chosen by the governor to create a new education plan. Have them think about issues that concern them, their classmates, their parents, and the community at large.
2. Have students write a short speech presenting their ideas to the governor. Urge them to be convincing in the presentation of their views.
3. Put all the student speeches together in a binder and make it available to school board members and the administration.

Discussion
1. What would you do differently in our school if you were the principal?
2. What is the best decision you have seen made at our school?
3. How can students get more involved in school decision making?

Enrichment
Encourage your students to attend a school board meeting. Make sure their opinions and ideas are heard. Give students the opportunity to interview candidates for administrative and teaching positions.

Market Yourself

Although high school students possess many wonderful skills, these skills often go unnoticed or unrecognized by teachers and administrators. It is important that students be given the chance to have their skills acknowledged. This activity motivates students to highlight their skills in a creative way.

Materials
▶ A guest recruiter

Instructions
1. Assign students the task of marketing themselves. Tell them a college or job recruiter is coming to visit the school and has asked that, instead of simply filling out an application, students market themselves.

2. Encourage students to be creative as they think about how they can best sell their skills and strengths. Tell them to be creative but not to lie about their skills when they speak to the recruiter.

3. Bring in the guest recruiter to hear the marketing pitches.

Discussion
1. Why is it so difficult to promote yourself?

2. What is your greatest asset?

3. How will this asset help you in the future?

Enrichment
Collect a variety of job and college applications and give one to each student. Help students sell themselves on paper, through their writing. Prompt them by asking a couple of questions: What is an effective way to get your strengths across to the person who is going to receive your application? How can you make sure all your accomplishments are brought to light?

ACTIVITY 5 Clay Models

Students of all ages love to play with different types of modeling clay. Clay is an effective medium that students can use to express themselves while having fun at the same time. This activity requires students to depict their answers to questions using modeling clay.

Materials ► Modeling clay

Instructions 1. Give students a healthy chunk of clay and inform them that they are going to be representing answers to questions with their clay. Tell them their clay models should be basic and also fun to design.

2. Have students use their modeling clay to depict, among other things, the following:

Their most cherished goal

Their thoughts on school

Their current mood

Their favorite expression

3. End the session by asking students to depict how they think the rest of their day will go.

Discussion 1. Is it easy or hard for you to think about your future? Explain.

2. What one goal do you want to achieve this year?

3. If you are unsuccessful at reaching your most important goal, what will you do?

Enrichment Ask students to create clay models representing who they are. The models should be abstract. Have students write a short essay explaining their artwork.

ACTIVITY 6 — Letter to the Editor

One effective way to have your opinions and ideas heard is to write a letter to the editor. Many people read the editorial pages of newspapers, and often a letter to the editor will shine light on an important issue. In this activity, students will be asked to write letters to the editor about an issue that concerns them.

Materials
- ► Editorial pages from various newspapers and magazines
- ► Writing paper and pencils or pens
- ► A notebook
- ► Envelopes and postage

Instructions
1. Have the students read a variety of editorials from magazines and newspapers: What are their thoughts on the editorials? Do they agree with them? In their view, what constitutes a good editorial?

2. Inform your students that they are going to write a letter to the editor about an issue that concerns them. Depending on the issue they select, the students will have to make an informed decision about where to send their letters. Students may choose the local newspaper, a paper from another state, or a magazine that reaches a nationwide audience.

3. Make photocopies of the students' letters and put them in the notebook so everyone in the class can read them.

4. Have students address their letters to the editor of the publication they have chosen and then mail them. Be sure to congratulate those students whose letters are published, and also display the newspapers or magazines that ran the letters.

Discussion
1. Why is it important for students to voice their opinions?
2. What constitutes a good editorial?
3. Why do people read editorials?

Enrichment
Encourage students to read the editorials in their local newspaper.

Use editorials as aids whenever you discuss current topics. How do the topics discussed in the editorials affect students, and what can students do to get involved?

Change the World

Today's students are the ones who will effect changes in the future of the world. It is therefore vital for students to understand that they have the power to change the world for the better. All they need is to believe in themselves and their abilities and then do something positive with their assets.

Materials
▸ The passage *Success*

Instructions
1. Read aloud to the class the following quote by the late, famed anthropologist Margaret Mead:

   "Never doubt that a small group of thoughtful, committed people can change the world. Indeed, it's the only thing that ever has."

2. Solicit students' reactions to and thoughts about Mead's comment on changing the world.

3. Ask students to share a quest with future generations: How can we change the world for the better?

4. Give students the passage *Success*. Although this passage is often attributed to Ralph Waldo Emerson, there is much debate as to whether Emerson actually wrote it. It is popular, and it is often quoted and posted on classroom and library walls.

5. Ask students to discuss with the class their thoughts on success.

Discussion
1. What does it mean to you to change the world?
2. What do you think you can accomplish with your life?
3. How do you define success?

Enrichment
Ask students to spend some time thinking about the meaning of success: Do they know someone who is successful? What makes this person successful? What three accomplishments in life would make a person successful?

Success

Success is to laugh often and much;
to win the respect of intelligent people and the
affection of children;
to earn the appreciation of honest critics and
endure the betrayal of false friends;
to appreciate beauty, to find the best in others;
to leave the world a bit better, whether by a healthy
child, a garden patch or a redeemed social
condition;
to know that even one life has breathed easier
because you lived;
this is to have succeeded.

Raising Student Aspirations: Classroom Activities for Grades 9–12
© 2003 by Russell J. Quaglia and Kristine M. Fox. Champaign, IL: Research Press (800) 519-2707

ACTIVITY 8   Scenarios for Confidence to Take Action

Read the following scenarios to your students one at a time. After you have read each scenario, give students ample time to think about their responses to it and then engage them in a lively class discussion.

1. Upon receiving this year's reading assignments, you and your classmates notice that you read several of the same books last year. The thought of studying these books again is agonizing. Some of your classmates are happy, though, because now they do not have to read a new book. What do you do?

2. You notice that a new student in the school is always being picked on. This girl does not hang out with you, so it would be much easier for you to look the other way. One day you walk into the bathroom and find her crying and obviously upset. Your friends just walk away. What do you do?

3. You notice that a nearby river has become so polluted that fish are turning up dead along the riverbank and there is an unusual odor. What can you do to ensure that your rivers are clean and safe?

Challenge Activities for Confidence to Take Action

For Students
- ► Challenge students to take a course that, because of its difficulty, they ordinarily would not take. Have them seek extra help and support when necessary.
- ► Challenge students to get involved in a club or a project that their friends might not think is cool, such as math club, an after-school choral group, or volunteer work at the nursing home.
- ► Challenge students to take the time to be nice to someone they think could use a friend.

For Teachers
- ► Share your skills at a staff meeting. Teach your colleagues about something you learned at a conference or workshop.
- ► Take the time to compliment your students and write notes on their essays and other written work—even on math exams.
- ► Get to know teachers from a different department. Learn about what they are doing and suggest ways for you to co-teach lessons.

About the Authors

Russell J. Quaglia, Ed.D., is the executive director of the Global Institute for Student Aspirations at Endicott College in Beverly, Massachusetts, and a professor of education. During an appearance on NBC TV's *Today Show,* he was described as America's foremost authority on the development and achievement of student aspirations.

A dynamic speaker, Dr. Quaglia travels extensively, presenting research-based information on student aspirations and motivation to audiences throughout the United States and around the world.

His opinions and comments on aspirations and controversial educational topics have been much sought after and published in national media such as the *Washington Post, Boston Globe, New York Times, USA Today, Chronicle of Higher Education,* and *Education Week.* He also has appeared on CNN and C-SPAN.

He received his bachelor's degree from Assumption College in Worcester, Massachusetts; a master of arts degree in economics from Boston College; and a master of education and doctorate from Columbia University, specializing in the area of organizational theory and behavior. Dr. Quaglia's research has been published in numerous professional journals, including *Research in Rural Education, Educational Administration Quarterly, Journal of Instructional Psychology, American School Board Journal, Adolescence,* and *Journal of Psychological and Educational Measurement.* His thoughts and opinions have also appeared in popular magazines such as *Reader's Digest, Better Homes and Gardens, Parent and Family,* and *Ladies' Home Journal.*

Kristine M. Fox is the director of field services for the Global Institute for Student Aspirations and an instructor at Endicott College. Most of her work involves teaching the importance of student aspirations to administrators, teachers, and students in schools throughout North America and abroad. In addition to working with these groups, she discusses with parents and other community members the significance of student aspirations.

She has presented extensively at conferences and workshops. She has conducted her site work throughout New England and also at a number of disparate locales such as Alaska, Arizona, Mexico, Toronto, and England.

She received her bachelor's degree from the University of Michigan and a master's degree in education from Harvard University. She has experience both as a classroom teacher and as a school administrator.